ODY, A. CHOCO

The Rise of Great Leaders From The Gboko Valley

First edition

This book was professionally typeset on Reedsy.
Find out more at reedsy.com

This book is dedicated to God.

Contents

Preface

The Rise of Great Leaders From The Gboko Valley is a powerful narrative that chronicles the transformation of a remote community into a beacon of progress, unity, and leadership. Set in the picturesque Gboko Valley, the story follows the journey of a young businessman, Ugo, and an elder, Nnadi, whose differing perspectives on change and tradition collide and ultimately merge to shape the valley's future.

Ugo, eager to modernize and bring industry to the valley, faces resistance from those who fear that change may erode the culture and values of the land. Nnadi, a wise elder, believes that the valley's strength lies in its rich traditions and cautions against rushing into change without preserving the essence of what has been built over generations. As tensions rise, the two leaders find common ground, working together to find solutions that honor the past while embracing the future.

Through their collaboration, the community learns to harness the best of both worlds—combining the wisdom of the elders with the innovation of the youth. The valley sees advancements in agriculture, technology, education, and infrastructure, all while maintaining a deep respect for its cultural heritage. The valley becomes a symbol of sustainable progress, where tradition and modernity coexist harmoniously.

The narrative unfolds over a series of events and milestones, highlighting the struggles, triumphs, and compromises that shape the valley's path. The leaders, young and old, guide their people through challenges, building a future that is rooted in shared values, mutual respect, and unity. In the end, the Gboko Valley emerges not only as a model of progress but as a testament to the power of collaboration, community, and the enduring strength of leadership that rises from within.

The Rise of Great Leaders From The Gboko Valley is a compelling tale of transformation, resilience, and the timeless importance of leadership that blends the past, present, and future to build a brighter tomorrow.

Acknowledgments

Thanks for your love and support.

1

Chapter 1

The Gboko Valley had always been a land steeped in history, a place where legends were born and great leaders were forged. Nestled between the towering hills and lush greenery of the Benue State, this valley was more than just a geographic feature. It was the cradle of dreams, a silent witness to the rise and fall of kingdoms, the strength of its people, and the resilience of their spirits. The sun, often fierce in its brightness, cast long shadows over the rich soil, which, in turn, bore the weight of centuries of struggle, triumph, and transformation.

In the heart of the valley, among the scattered villages, one could hear the echoes of ancestors speaking through the wind, the rustling of the trees, and the rhythmic sound of drums that resonated deep within the bones of those who heard them. These were not just the sounds of celebration or mourning; they were the call to duty, the pulse of a community that had always known how to rise above its challenges. But it was the stories of those who stood as beacons of leadership—those who had navigated the path to greatness—that truly defined the valley.

The story of leadership in the Gboko Valley was not one of inherited power or mere political maneuvering. It was a story of individuals who rose from humble beginnings, faced immense obstacles, and overcame them through sheer determination and vision. Their journeys were shaped by the land itself, by the trials of survival, by the strength of community, and by the unrelenting pursuit of justice and equality. Each leader that emerged from this valley did so with the understanding that they were part of something much larger than themselves—a greater purpose that would transcend time and place.

As the years passed, the valley became a magnet for those seeking to understand the essence of leadership. It was said that one could not truly lead unless they had walked the rugged paths of Gboko, tasted the bitter winds that swept across its plains, and heard the wisdom that whispered in the silence of its nights. These leaders did not rise to prominence through manipulation or deceit; they rose through action, through the ability to unite people, through the pursuit of what was right even when the road was difficult and uncertain.

The first among them was a man whose name had become synonymous with courage and vision—Okwu. Born into a family of farmers, Okwu's early life was marked by struggle. His parents, simple people who worked the land with their hands, struggled to make ends meet, but they instilled in him the value of hard work, integrity, and humility. Okwu was a child of the land, his hands strong from years of labor in the fields, and his heart filled with the wisdom passed down through generations. Yet, it was his mind that set him apart, a mind that was always seeking to understand more, to find better ways to help his people thrive.

He was not the tallest or the most physically imposing of his peers, but there was something magnetic about him. People listened when he spoke, not because of his loudness or forceful tone, but because of the conviction in his voice. He was a natural leader, one who led not by command but by example. His first act of leadership came when a drought threatened the livelihoods of the villagers. While others were content to wait for help from the outside, Okwu took action. He led a group of villagers to dig a well, drawing water from deep below the surface. It was grueling work, but he did not hesitate, even when the task seemed impossible. Under his guidance, the well was completed, and the community had water once more. This simple yet profound act of service would define his legacy, and the people of Gboko would forever remember the day when their leader showed them the power of perseverance.

Years later, after Okwu's death, the valley would witness the rise of another leader—Ameh, a woman whose strength was not just in her physical presence but in her ability to empathize with the struggles of others. Ameh's leadership was tested in a time of great division, when the valley was torn between rival factions vying for control. She emerged not from the political elite, but from the common people, and her ascension to power was anything but conventional. She was not born into wealth or privilege, but she was born with a deep sense of justice and an unyielding belief in the power of unity.

Ameh's journey to leadership was fraught with challenges. As a young woman, she faced many barriers—cultural norms that sought to silence her voice, societal expectations that sought to limit her ambition. But Ameh refused to be confined by these limitations. She saw the fractures within her community, the petty rivalries that threatened to tear it apart, and she knew that something had to be done. She began by speaking to the people, not in grand speeches, but in the quiet moments, in the small gatherings, and in the homes of those who felt forgotten by the system. She listened to their stories, their pains, their hopes. It was in these conversations that she found her strength, for she understood that true leadership came from understanding and connection, not from authority or coercion.

Under her leadership, the rival factions that once fought bitterly against each other found common ground. Ameh was a master of negotiation, a peacemaker whose ability to unite people was unparalleled. She did not promise to end all the problems of the valley, but she promised to lead with empathy, to ensure that no one would be left behind. Her leadership was marked by the creation of initiatives that focused on education, healthcare, and economic development. She championed the cause of women, ensuring that they had equal access to opportunities and platforms to voice their concerns. Under her rule, the Gboko Valley flourished, not just in material wealth, but in social cohesion and unity.

But it was not just Okwu and Ameh who left their mark on the valley. There were others, too, leaders whose names might not have been as widely known but whose contributions were no less significant. There was Tsegba, a man who understood the importance of knowledge and education. His vision for the valley was one where every child had access to quality education, where

4

the youth were equipped with the tools they needed to build a better future. Tsegba's passion for learning was infectious, and under his leadership, schools were established, scholarships were created, and a generation of young people was empowered to pursue their dreams.

Then there was Uka, a leader whose legacy lay in the realm of agriculture. Uka understood that the strength of the valley lay in its ability to feed itself, to harness the land's resources for the benefit of all. He introduced innovative farming techniques, bringing prosperity to the valley's farmers and ensuring that food security was never again a concern. His policies were far-reaching, transforming the landscape of agriculture in Gboko, and his name became synonymous with progress in the sector.

Through each of these leaders, the Gboko Valley had proven time and time again that true leadership was not about titles or power; it was about service, sacrifice, and the relentless pursuit of the greater good. The valley had produced men and women who had led not for personal gain, but for the collective well-being of their people. Their legacies lived on in the stories told by the elders, in the lessons taught to the children, and in the community that thrived because of their unwavering commitment to the betterment of all.

As the sun set on the Gboko Valley, casting its golden glow over the land, one could not help but feel the presence of those great leaders who had come before. Their spirits were in the air, in the earth, and in the very fabric of the community. The valley had been shaped by their hands, and the future would be shaped by the lessons they had left behind. Their rise was not just the rise of individuals; it was the rise of a people, a testament to the strength of the human spirit and the power of leadership rooted in love, service, and a deep connection to the land.

2

Chapter 2

The Gboko Valley had been known for many things—the lush soil, the wide plains, the winding rivers, and, most of all, the leaders it produced. But the greatness of these leaders did not come from their birthright or any external privilege. It came from their ability to transform the challenges of their time into opportunities for growth, unity, and progress. And, as the world continued to change, the legacy of these leaders would inspire generations to come.

One such leader was Makurdi, a man whose life would become a testament to the power of resilience and determination. Born in a small village on the outskirts of the Gboko Valley, Makurdi's early life was one filled with hardship. His parents, though loving and hardworking, had little to offer in terms of material wealth. Yet, they imbued him with an invaluable asset—the belief that a person's worth was determined not by what they had, but by who they were. Makurdi took these lessons to heart, and as he grew, he sought out opportunities to make a difference in his community. His path to leadership, however, was neither easy nor straightforward.

In his youth, Makurdi was often overlooked. He was not the most charismatic, nor did he possess the outward qualities that one might expect of a leader. He was quiet and reserved, often spending his time reading books and contemplating the world around him. It was in these moments of solitude that he began to develop his vision for a better future. He saw the vast potential of the Gboko Valley, not just in terms of its resources, but in the people who lived there. They were a people of immense strength and wisdom, but they lacked the unity and direction to harness their collective power.

Makurdi believed that true leadership was not about imposing one's will on others, but about inspiring them to see their own potential and to work together for a common goal. It was a lesson he had learned from his parents, who had taught him that the strength of a community lies in the strength of its individuals, and that true greatness comes not from selfish ambition, but from serving others. With this understanding in mind, Makurdi set out to become a leader who would help his people realize their collective potential.

He began by focusing on education. In a region where access to formal schooling was limited, Makurdi understood that the future of the valley depended on empowering the youth. He worked tirelessly to establish schools, secure funding for teachers, and create programs that would provide the younger generation with the tools they needed to succeed. His efforts were not without resistance. Many were skeptical of his vision, believing that education was a luxury that could not be afforded in a region where survival was often a daily struggle. But Makurdi refused to back down. He knew that the key to unlocking the valley's potential lay in the minds of its youth.

Slowly but surely, Makurdi's vision began to take shape. The schools he had helped to establish began to flourish, and the children who attended them were provided with opportunities they had never before dreamed possible. As the number of educated youth grew, so too did the community's sense of pride and purpose. They began to realize that they were capable of more than just surviving; they were capable of thriving. This realization sparked a wave of progress throughout the valley, and Makurdi's influence began to spread.

But Makurdi's journey was not without its challenges. As his influence grew, so did the opposition. There were those who felt threatened by his ideas and who sought to undermine his efforts. Political factions within the valley began to vie for control, and soon, Makurdi found himself at the center of a fierce battle for leadership. It was a battle not of armies or weapons, but of ideologies. Makurdi's vision of unity and progress clashed with the traditional power structures that had long held sway in the valley.

Yet, Makurdi did not fight with anger or bitterness. He understood that true leadership came not from defeating one's opponents, but from finding common ground. He reached out to those who opposed him, seeking to understand their concerns and to find ways to address them. His ability to listen, to empathize, and to seek compromise earned him the respect of even his fiercest critics. Slowly, but surely, he was able to bridge the divides that had once threatened to tear the community apart.

One of the most defining moments of Makurdi's leadership came during a time of crisis. A severe drought had ravaged the valley, threatening the livelihoods of thousands. The crops had withered, and the rivers had dried up. People were desperate, and tensions were running high. It was during this time that

Makurdi's leadership truly shone. Rather than succumb to panic or despair, he remained calm and focused. He organized a relief effort that brought together people from all corners of the valley. They worked together to build irrigation systems, to gather resources, and to provide food and water to those in need.

The drought lasted for months, but under Makurdi's guidance, the valley was able to weather the storm. The relief effort not only alleviated the immediate crisis, but it also brought the community closer together. People from all walks of life, from farmers to merchants to educators, came together to support one another. It was a powerful reminder of what could be accomplished when people set aside their differences and worked towards a common goal.

As the years passed, Makurdi's influence continued to grow. His legacy was not just in the institutions he helped to build, or the programs he put in place, but in the spirit of cooperation and unity that he fostered within the valley. He had shown the people of Gboko that they were not alone, that they were stronger when they worked together. And though he was no longer the young man who had first set out to change his community, his vision remained just as powerful.

Makurdi's leadership was marked by humility and selfless-ness. He never sought power for its own sake, and he never used his position to enrich himself. Instead, he viewed his role as a servant to the people, a guide who could help them achieve their potential. And as the valley continued to grow and evolve, it became clear that the lessons of Makurdi's leadership had left an indelible mark on the land.

In the years following his passing, the people of Gboko continued to honor his memory. They carried forward the values he had instilled in them—the importance of education, the power of unity, and the belief that true leadership comes from service. And though the valley produced many more leaders in the years to come, none would ever quite match the impact of Makurdi.

The rise of leaders in the Gboko Valley was not simply the rise of individuals; it was the rise of a community that understood the importance of working together for the common good. It was the rise of a people who had learned that greatness was not measured by wealth or power, but by the ability to inspire others to reach their full potential. And as the valley continued to thrive, the legacy of its great leaders lived on, shaping the future for generations to come.

In the end, the story of the rise of great leaders from the Gboko Valley was a story of hope—a hope that the power of unity, the strength of community, and the vision of those who dare to dream could overcome any obstacle. It was a story that would be told for generations, reminding the people of the valley that greatness is not given, but earned through hard work, sacrifice, and a deep love for one's people. And as long as the winds blew through the valley, and the rivers flowed through its lands, the lessons of those great leaders would continue to inspire all who called it home.

3

Chapter 3

The people of the Gboko Valley had long been known for their strength and resilience, but few would ever forget the remarkable leadership that emerged from the valley during times of strife. It was a place where men and women rose above the harshest circumstances to forge a future that was brighter than the adversity they faced. In the heart of this valley, the stories of leadership, perseverance, and unity were written by those who dared to dream big, even when the world seemed to conspire against them.

Among these great figures was Adama, a woman whose name would forever be synonymous with courage and vision. Adama was born into a community that, like many others in the valley, had struggled to overcome the many obstacles nature and history had thrown at it. Her village, perched on the edge of the fertile plains, had witnessed both prosperity and hardship. The seasons were often unpredictable, and the roads that led to the village were treacherous, especially in times of heavy rainfall. For years, Adama's village had been isolated, struggling to make its way in the world while the leaders of surrounding areas grew stronger and wealthier.

Yet, there was something different about Adama from the moment she was born. She was the daughter of a respected elder, known for his wisdom and insight, but it was Adama's passion for learning that set her apart. While other children played in the fields, she could be found perched beneath the large mango tree, reading the few books her father had managed to procure from traders passing through the valley. She learned quickly, soaking in the lessons of history, politics, and the world beyond her village.

Her mind was sharp, and she could see things that others could not. Where many saw only the endless cycle of struggle and hardship, Adama saw opportunity. She saw potential in the land, in the people, and most importantly, in herself. As she grew older, Adama began to share her vision with others. She spoke of the need for unity, for collaboration, and for breaking free from the patterns that had kept them shackled in a state of poverty and isolation. Her words were powerful, and slowly, the people of her village began to take notice.

But change, as always, was not easy. Many were skeptical of her ideas, clinging to the belief that their traditional ways were enough to sustain them. They had always relied on their own resources, their own hands, and their own wisdom. They didn't need outside influence, they argued. They didn't need to be involved in the world beyond the valley. But Adama was not deterred. She knew that survival alone was not enough. The people needed to thrive, not just survive. And so, she set out to bring about the change that was needed, no matter the cost.

Adama's journey to leadership began with education. She knew that in order to lift her people out of ignorance, she needed to start by educating the youth. The elders were set in their ways, but the children, the future of the valley, were still malleable. Adama began by gathering the young people of the village, teaching them not only the traditional knowledge of the land, but also the broader world of science, mathematics, and literature. She brought in traveling teachers who could help her create a system of education that would challenge the conventional wisdom of her time.

But education was just the beginning. Adama also saw the need for infrastructure. Her village had always struggled with basic resources—clean water, roads, healthcare. These were fundamental issues that no leader before her had been able to address. In a region where the lack of proper roads often meant isolation during the rainy season, Adama knew that her village had to connect to the outside world if they were to ever prosper. She began to gather resources, rallying her people to build the roads that would link them to other villages and towns. The task was immense, and at times it seemed impossible, but Adama's determination and leadership never wavered.

The road project became a symbol of what could be accomplished when people worked together. Despite the challenges, the villagers built the road with their own hands, working day and night, hauling stones and gravel, and slowly transforming the once impassable terrain into a pathway that would connect them to the outside world. The road was not just a physical structure;

it was a testament to the strength of the community, and to Adama's ability to inspire and unite people behind a common cause.

As the road was completed, Adama turned her attention to other matters. She recognized the importance of agriculture in the valley and knew that if her people were to thrive, they needed to improve their farming methods. With the help of the young people she had educated, she introduced new farming techniques, including crop rotation, irrigation systems, and the planting of more resilient crops. The valley, once dependent on only a few crops, began to flourish with a variety of produce. The farmers, once skeptical of change, began to see the benefits of Adama's vision, and soon the entire community was reaping the rewards of the new farming practices.

But it wasn't just the land and the resources that were changing in the Gboko Valley. The people were changing, too. Adama's leadership had inspired a shift in mindset. The villagers began to believe that they could achieve more than they ever thought possible. They saw that with education, collaboration, and a willingness to embrace change, they could overcome any obstacle. As the valley's prosperity grew, so did the sense of pride among the people. They were no longer just survivors; they were thrivers, and Adama was the leader who had shown them the way.

However, leadership in the Gboko Valley was never without its challenges. As the valley began to prosper, it attracted the attention of neighboring villages and leaders who felt threatened by Adama's rise. They had long held power over the region and viewed her success as a challenge to their authority. Soon, Adama found herself facing opposition from powerful figures who sought to undermine her efforts. These leaders, who had once been allies, turned against her, using political maneuvering and threats to try to stifle her progress.

But Adama was not a woman to be easily intimidated. She knew that the true strength of her leadership came not from her position of power, but from the people who stood with her. She turned to her community once again, rallying them to defend the progress they had made. It was a tense time, but through careful negotiation, diplomacy, and the support of her people, Adama was able to protect the advancements she had brought to the valley.

In the face of opposition, Adama's resolve only grew stronger. She understood that leadership was not about avoiding conflict, but about facing it head-on with the strength of conviction and the courage to stand for what was right. She used this period of challenge to solidify her position as a leader not only within the Gboko Valley, but also in the larger region. Her reputation as a wise, compassionate, and resolute leader spread far beyond the valley, earning her respect from other leaders who had once viewed her with skepticism.

Adama's legacy, like that of many great leaders, was built not on the battles she fought, but on the lives she touched. Her leadership transformed the Gboko Valley from a place of isolation and poverty into a thriving, prosperous community. The changes she implemented were not just in the physical infrastructure or the agricultural practices, but in the hearts and minds of the people she led. She had shown them that leadership was about vision, courage, and the ability to inspire others to reach their fullest potential.

As the years went by, Adama's name became synonymous with greatness in the Gboko Valley. The roads she built, the schools she founded, and the unity she forged among her people were all enduring symbols of her leadership. And though her time as a leader came to an end, the principles she instilled in the valley lived on, guiding future generations of leaders to rise to the challenges of their time.

The story of Adama was not just the story of one woman, but of an entire community that had risen together to create a better future. It was a story of vision, resilience, and the power of leadership to transform lives. And as long as the sun continued to shine over the Gboko Valley, her legacy would live on, a testament to the greatness that could emerge from even the most unlikely of places.

4

Chapter 4

The story of leadership in the Gboko Valley did not end with Adama, nor did her achievements mark the final chapter of the valley's remarkable journey. The foundation she built, however, would set the stage for future generations to rise to the challenges of their time, carrying forward her legacy of unity, progress, and resilience. It was a legacy that would inspire not just those who knew her but countless others who would look to the valley as an example of what could be achieved through collective effort and visionary leadership.

Years passed, and the world outside the valley continued to change. The global landscape was evolving, shaped by forces both known and unknown. The political environment was shifting, new technologies were emerging, and the economy was being redefined in ways that seemed impossible to predict. But in the Gboko Valley, the lessons of Adama's leadership remained etched in the hearts of those who had witnessed her rise to power and success. And it was from this community, nurtured by her wisdom, that the next great leader would emerge.

This leader was Kelechi, a young man born at a time when the valley was beginning to reap the rewards of the work that had been done. He grew up surrounded by the stories of his people—stories of hardship and triumph, of visionaries who had risen from the dust to lead their people toward a better future. Kelechi's own father had been a prominent member of the village council during Adama's time and had played a key role in helping to shape the valley's transformation. From a young age, Kelechi was taught the values of integrity, hard work, and the importance of serving the greater good.

But unlike many of his peers, Kelechi was not content to simply live in the shadow of those who had come before him. He recognized that the world was changing at an unprecedented rate, and while the progress of the valley was undeniable, he knew that the time had come for a new kind of leadership—one that would not only honor the legacy of the past but also embrace the opportunities and challenges of the future.

Kelechi's vision was clear: the valley needed to evolve once again. While Adama's leadership had been marked by physical infrastructure and agricultural reforms, Kelechi knew that the next step would require a focus on innovation, technology, and sustainable growth. The valley, now a thriving community, could no longer afford to rely solely on the methods of the past. The world was moving faster than ever, and the people of the valley had to move with it.

But Kelechi's vision was not without its own challenges. As he sought to introduce new ideas and foster a culture of innovation, he encountered resistance from those who were still deeply attached to the traditions of the past. Many saw Kelechi's emphasis on technology and change as a threat to the values that had brought them success. The elders, who had lived through the transformative years of Adama's leadership, were particularly wary of the rapid pace at which the world seemed to be advancing. To them, the future was uncertain, and they clung to the comfort of the tried-and-true methods that had served their people for generations.

However, Kelechi was not easily dissuaded. He understood that leadership was not about imposing change on others; it was about inspiring people to see the potential in new ideas. And so, he began to speak to the people of the valley not just as a leader but as a fellow traveler on a journey toward a better future. He made it clear that the foundation of Adama's leadership—the unity, the strength, the sense of community—would remain intact. But he also emphasized that in order to thrive in the modern world, the valley needed to adapt.

Kelechi's first major initiative was focused on education. While Adama's focus had been on providing basic education to the youth of the valley, Kelechi understood that the future required more than just literacy and arithmetic. The world was moving toward an age of technology, and the valley needed to prepare its youth for this new reality. He worked with local educators and brought in experts from outside the valley to develop a curriculum that would equip the next generation with the skills they would need to succeed in a rapidly changing world.

At first, there was some skepticism. Many of the elders were unsure about the value of this new education, which they saw as impractical and disconnected from the realities of life in the valley. But Kelechi was patient, knowing that change would take time. He began by introducing small pilot programs, focusing on teaching basic skills in computer literacy and entrepreneurship. These programs were initially met with resistance, but slowly, the young people of the valley began to see the benefits of this new education. They saw how it could open doors to new opportunities, how it could connect them to the world beyond their borders.

The success of these early programs was a turning point for Kelechi. He had shown that change could be embraced without sacrificing the values that had made the valley great. Slowly, more and more people began to see the potential of the new approach. Parents, once reluctant to send their children to these modern schools, began to recognize that the future was not just about farming and tradition—it was about adaptability, creativity, and the ability to solve the problems of a rapidly changing world.

Kelechi's next focus was on agriculture. While Adama's reforms had revolutionized farming techniques in the valley, Kelechi knew that sustainability was the key to long-term success. He introduced new farming practices that focused on conserving the environment, reducing waste, and making use of renewable resources. He also began to encourage the development of agricultural technologies that would help farmers improve crop yields while using fewer resources. In particular, Kelechi was a strong advocate for the use of solar-powered irrigation systems, which would help farmers reduce their dependence on unpredictable rainfall and conserve water.

Once again, the elders were skeptical. They had spent their entire lives relying on traditional methods, and they were unsure about the newfangled technology that Kelechi was advocating. But as with his educational initiatives, Kelechi took a patient approach. He worked with the farmers, showing them how these new techniques could actually increase their yields and improve their quality of life. Over time, more and more farmers embraced the new methods, and the valley's agricultural output grew exponentially. The people of the valley began to realize that Kelechi's leadership was not about discarding the old ways—it was about enhancing them with new tools and ideas.

One of Kelechi's greatest accomplishments was his ability to foster a spirit of collaboration and innovation. He understood that the future of the valley depended not just on technological advancements but on the ability of the people to work together toward common goals. Under his leadership, the valley became a hub for innovation, attracting entrepreneurs, thinkers, and creators from all over the region. The once-isolated valley had transformed into a vibrant community where ideas were exchanged freely, and collaboration was seen as the key to progress.

But Kelechi's leadership was not without its challenges. As the valley grew, it attracted the attention of outside forces— companies, governments, and individuals who sought to profit from the valley's newfound prosperity. Some of these outside forces were well-intentioned, seeking to partner with the valley and share in its success. But others had more selfish motives, hoping to exploit the valley's resources for their own gain.

Kelechi found himself at the center of a delicate balancing act. He had to navigate the complex world of politics and business while ensuring that the valley's interests were protected. He was committed to ensuring that the people of the valley would benefit from the prosperity they had worked so hard to achieve, and he worked tirelessly to negotiate fair deals with outside partners. But even as he faced these external pressures, Kelechi remained steadfast in his commitment to the people of the valley. His leadership was defined not by the accolades he received or the power he wielded but by his unwavering dedication to his community.

The story of Kelechi's rise to leadership is one of vision, perseverance, and the ability to unite people around a common cause. It is a story of how the valley, once known for its isolation and poverty, transformed into a thriving community that embraced change while honoring its roots. Kelechi's leadership was a continuation of Adama's legacy, but it was also something new—something that looked toward the future while never forgetting the past. The Gboko Valley had become a place where leadership was not defined by titles or positions of power but by the ability to inspire others to believe in their potential and work together to create a better world.

5

Chapter 5

The story of the Gboko Valley was no longer just about one leader's rise, nor was it limited to the struggles of the past. By the time the fifth chapter of the valley's tale began, a new era had dawned. It was an era shaped by the work of those who had gone before, their struggles, and their triumphs. But it was also an era that promised something new—a future that had yet to be fully written. The landscape of the valley, while much more developed, still carried within it the essence of its origins— the sense of resilience, unity, and determination that had been passed down through generations.

The next leader to rise in the Gboko Valley was someone not entirely unfamiliar to the valley's people. Nnena was the daughter of a well-respected elder who had contributed greatly to the community's success. Her upbringing had been steeped in the values of leadership—integrity, service, and a deep understanding of the land and the people. From a young age, Nnena showed remarkable intelligence and a unique ability to empathize with others. She was a listener, always paying attention to the concerns of her peers, the elders, and even the youngest members of the community. People trusted her because she didn't seek power for its own sake; instead, she wanted to see her people grow and thrive.

As a young woman, Nnena was given the responsibility of assisting with the management of the valley's resources. It was a position that had traditionally been filled by men, but Nnena had proven herself capable, making decisions that improved efficiency and ensured that the valley's resources were managed wisely. Under her leadership, the valley had grown prosperous. However, despite the progress, challenges still loomed on the horizon.

Nnena was keenly aware of the shifting dynamics of the world around her. The world outside the valley was advancing rapidly in ways that the people of the Gboko Valley had never imagined. Urbanization, globalization, and the spread of technology had brought both opportunities and challenges to the doorsteps of rural communities. While the valley was far from untouched, there was still a sense of isolation—a belief that the world outside was moving at a pace that would leave them behind if they did not act quickly.

One of Nnena's first actions as a leader was to address the growing gap between the valley and the outside world. She understood that the valley had to become a center for innovation, not just a place where old ways of living persisted. At the same time, she did not want to abandon the values and traditions that had defined the valley's character for centuries. She envisioned a world in which the old and new could coexist, where the people of

25

the valley could harness the power of modernity without losing sight of the deep cultural roots that had anchored them.

The first step toward this vision was revitalizing the valley's economy. Agriculture had long been the backbone of the community, but Nnena recognized that the world's agricultural landscape was changing. The global market for goods was becoming more competitive, and small-scale farmers could no longer afford to rely solely on traditional farming methods. There was a need for technological innovation, new farming techniques, and, most importantly, access to markets that were not limited to the immediate surrounding regions.

With the help of her advisors, Nnena sought to introduce new farming technologies—tools that would help the valley's farmers improve their productivity while also making their work more sustainable. She introduced irrigation systems powered by renewable energy, which would allow farmers to grow crops year-round, even during the dry season. Additionally, she encouraged the use of organic farming practices, which would not only improve the quality of the crops but also reduce their environmental impact. This approach, though met with some resistance, eventually gained traction, especially as farmers began to see the tangible benefits of adopting these new methods.

Alongside agricultural innovation, Nnena was keenly aware of the importance of education in this new era. While the valley had made great strides in education under previous leaders, Nnena knew that there was still work to be done. The youth of the valley needed to be equipped with the skills and knowledge to compete in an increasingly globalized world. She spearheaded the creation of schools that not only focused on traditional subjects like literacy and math but also offered courses in science, technology, and business. The curriculum was designed to inspire critical thinking, problem-solving, and innovation. Nnena's goal was to ensure that the young people of the Gboko Valley were not just passive recipients of knowledge but active participants in shaping their future.

One of the greatest challenges Nnena faced during her leadership was balancing the demands of modernization with the preservation of the valley's rich cultural heritage. The people of the valley were proud of their traditions, and many feared that the rapid changes would lead to the erosion of their cultural identity. Nnena understood these concerns deeply. She knew that cultural pride was a cornerstone of the valley's unity and strength. And so, she made it a priority to integrate the valley's traditions into the modern world, rather than allowing them to be discarded or forgotten.

She encouraged local artists, musicians, and storytellers to share their work with the younger generation. She helped to establish cultural centers where people could come together to learn about their history, participate in traditional ceremonies, and preserve the oral traditions that had been passed down through generations. Nnena also ensured that these cultural elements were woven into the education system, ensuring that the youth of the valley understood the value of their heritage while being prepared for the demands of the modern world.

As Nnena continued her efforts to bring about positive change in the Gboko Valley, her leadership was not without its critics.

Some of the older members of the community were hesitant to embrace the new direction she was leading them in, fearing that it would threaten the core values they had fought so hard to preserve. However, Nnena's calm demeanor and her unwavering commitment to her people won over most of the skeptics. She demonstrated time and again that she was not seeking to impose change for its own sake but rather to build upon the foundation of what had come before.

Over time, the fruits of Nnena's leadership began to show. The valley's agricultural output increased significantly, and the people began to see the tangible benefits of modern farming techniques. The schools flourished, producing a new generation of leaders, entrepreneurs, and professionals who were ready to take on the world. The valley's economy grew stronger, and its people felt empowered by the knowledge that they were no longer just passive observers of change but active participants in shaping their own future.

But perhaps the most lasting legacy of Nnena's leadership was the sense of unity that she fostered within the valley. In a time when the world was becoming more fragmented, Nnena understood that the strength of the valley lay in its people's ability to work together, to respect their differences, and to find common ground. Under her leadership, the people of the Gboko Valley learned that they could embrace change without losing their sense of identity, and they could move forward into the future while holding on to the values that had made them strong.

As Nnena's leadership came to an end, the Gboko Valley stood as a shining example of what could be accomplished when a community came together under the guidance of a visionary leader. The valley, once a remote and isolated region, had transformed into a thriving, innovative, and united community. The people of the Gboko Valley had learned that true leadership was not about power or control, but about empowering others and working together to create a better future. And in this new chapter of their story, they knew that the rise of great leaders would never end—it was a cycle that would continue for generations to come.

6

Chapter 6

The Gboko Valley had always been a land of potential, but it wasn't until the rise of the next leader that the full scope of its promise began to unfold. Chapter six of the valley's story marked a pivotal moment. The events leading up to this moment had tested the resilience of its people, but they were on the cusp of something greater. The land, its resources, and its people were all poised for growth—but it would take more than just the knowledge of the old ways to secure the future. It would take courage, vision, and an unwavering belief in the possibilities ahead.

Bello, a man who had grown up amidst the people of the valley, was the leader who would carry the weight of these expectations. He was not a typical leader, one who came from a long line of political rulers or wealthy families. Instead, Bello's background was humble. He was the son of a farmer and a teacher, someone who had learned the values of hard work and service early in life. From the time he was a child, Bello showed an interest in the world beyond the valley, studying books on leadership, economics, and science. He spent countless hours learning from the elders, listening to their stories and absorbing their wisdom. He knew that for the valley to continue to grow, it would have to adapt to the modern world without losing its soul.

Bello's leadership journey began when he became involved in local governance. His desire to help his community was rooted in a deep understanding of its needs. The valley had made significant progress, especially under Nnena's guidance, but there were still gaps to be filled. The infrastructure needed improvements, education was still limited to certain areas, and the economy, while growing, had not reached its full potential. Most importantly, the younger generation needed a direction— a sense of purpose that would carry them into the future.

When he assumed leadership, Bello immediately recognized that his first task was to unite the people. The valley had prospered, but in many ways, it had become fragmented. Different sectors of society were advancing at different rates, and there was a need for cohesion. His leadership would not only have to focus on economic development and modernization but also on healing the divisions that had cropped up within the community.

One of Bello's first decisions was to convene a gathering of all the valley's stakeholders: the elders, community leaders, farmers, teachers, and young people. He knew that true progress could only be achieved if everyone had a voice in the conversation. This gathering was unlike any that had taken place before. It was a true representation of the valley's diversity, and it allowed the people to come together in a spirit of collaboration. Rather than focusing on differences, Bello encouraged a conversation that centered on shared goals and collective responsibility.

The discussions were intense and at times emotional. People voiced their concerns about the changing world and what it meant for the future of the valley. Some were excited about the possibilities of technology and modernization, while others feared the loss of their traditional ways of life. Farmers expressed concerns about the impact of new agricultural techniques on their land, and educators talked about the challenges of teaching in a world where the younger generation seemed distracted by new forms of entertainment.

Bello listened carefully, weighing every opinion and seeking common ground. He was a patient leader, understanding that true leadership required not just making decisions but also making people feel heard. After several days of dialogue, the gathering concluded with a set of shared goals for the valley's future. These goals included investing in education, improving infrastructure, fostering economic development, and ensuring that cultural traditions remained an integral part of life in the valley.

One of the most important steps in this new chapter of the valley's story was the establishment of a comprehensive education reform program. Bello understood that the world was changing rapidly, and the valley's young people needed to be prepared to meet those changes head-on. The schools were expanded, and new curricula were developed that combined traditional teachings with modern knowledge. This approach was designed to bridge the gap between the old and the new, ensuring that the youth of the valley would be able to contribute to the global economy while also preserving the cultural values that had made the valley strong.

At the same time, Bello recognized that the valley's infrastructure needed urgent attention. Roads, transportation, and communication systems were all lacking, which hampered trade and limited the region's access to wider markets. Under his leadership, major investments were made in infrastructure. New roads were built, linking the valley to neighboring regions, and bridges were constructed to connect remote areas. These improvements facilitated the transportation of goods and made it easier for people to travel for work, education, and healthcare. The valley became more accessible, and the economy flourished as a result.

However, Bello's leadership was not without its challenges. As the valley's population grew, so too did the pressure on its resources. The demand for food, water, and energy increased, and environmental concerns became a pressing issue. Bello knew that the valley's natural resources were finite, and he was determined to find sustainable solutions to meet the needs of the growing population without damaging the environment.

In response, he implemented a series of green initiatives designed to reduce the valley's carbon footprint and promote environmental stewardship. He encouraged the use of renewable energy sources, such as solar and wind power, and introduced water conservation measures that would ensure the long-term availability of clean water. He also promoted organic farming practices, which helped to maintain soil health and protect the surrounding ecosystem.

These efforts were met with resistance from some quarters, particularly among those who had always relied on traditional methods of farming. However, Bello was resolute in his belief that the valley's future depended on sustainability. He worked closely with local farmers to demonstrate the benefits of these new methods, and over time, they began to see the advantages of environmentally friendly practices.

As Bello continued to push for progress, he never lost sight of the importance of unity. He understood that leadership was about more than just making decisions—it was about bringing people together and creating a sense of shared purpose. One of the most significant achievements of his leadership was the creation of a community development council that brought together leaders from all walks of life. This council became a forum for discussion, problem-solving, and collaboration, ensuring that the voices of the people were always heard.

By the time Bello's leadership came to an end, the valley had undergone a transformation. It was no longer a place defined solely by its history or its reliance on tradition. The valley had evolved into a thriving, modern community that balanced progress with preservation. Bello had succeeded in creating an environment in which the people could grow, adapt, and prosper while remaining deeply connected to their roots.

As Bello passed the mantle of leadership to the next generation, he could take pride in the knowledge that he had played a pivotal role in shaping the valley's future. His leadership had been defined by his ability to listen, to unite, and to guide the people of the valley toward a common goal. The rise of great leaders from the Gboko Valley was not just about individuals—it was about the collective strength and vision of a community determined to build a better tomorrow.

The legacy of Bello and those who had come before him would continue to inspire future generations. The valley had become a place where leadership was not defined by power, but by the ability to bring people together and create positive change. And as the people of the Gboko Valley looked toward the future, they knew that the rise of great leaders was a story that would never end.

7

Chapter 7

The Gboko Valley had always been a place where tradition and progress coexisted in a delicate balance, but as the years passed, the winds of change began to blow stronger. The future of the valley seemed to depend not only on its natural resources but on the willingness of its people to embrace the new while holding tightly to the old. Chapter seven marked the beginning of a new era, one that would test the valley's strength in ways it had never been tested before.

Under the leadership of the new generation, the valley had flourished in many areas. Education was more accessible, infrastructure was improving, and the economy was booming. Yet, the rapid development came with its own set of challenges. The fast pace of modernization brought with it the danger of losing the cultural identity that had made the valley so special in the first place. The youth, in particular, were caught between the demands of the modern world and the traditions of their ancestors. The leadership, now under the direction of Amina, recognized that the valley's future depended on finding a way to bridge this gap.

Amina was no stranger to the struggles of leadership. A native of the valley, she had witnessed firsthand the struggles of her people and had always dreamed of making a difference. Her background in law and social justice had shaped her understanding of what was needed to lead effectively. When she took on the mantle of leadership, she knew that it was her responsibility to ensure that the valley's development did not come at the cost of its cultural integrity. Amina understood that her role was not just to guide the valley into the future but to ensure that its past was not forgotten in the rush toward progress.

One of Amina's first acts as leader was to convene a series of town hall meetings across the valley. She wanted to hear directly from the people, to understand their concerns and ideas for the future. The meetings were well-attended, and the people spoke candidly about the changes they were experiencing. Many expressed excitement about the new opportunities that modernization had brought, while others feared that the valley's identity was being eroded. Farmers worried that traditional agricultural practices were being replaced by commercial farming methods, and elders expressed concern about the loss of indigenous languages and customs.

Amina listened carefully to every concern and understood the need for balance. She knew that the valley's strength lay in its ability to blend the old with the new, to preserve the traditions that had shaped its people while embracing the opportunities that modernity offered. The question, however, was how to make this vision a reality.

She decided that the first step in bridging the gap between tradition and progress was to create a cultural preservation program. The goal was to ensure that the younger generation would have access to the rich history and traditions of the valley while still being prepared for the challenges of the modern world. Amina worked with local educators, historians, and cultural leaders to develop a curriculum that would teach the valley's history, language, art, and traditions alongside modern subjects like science, technology, and economics.

The program was designed to be flexible, allowing students to learn about their heritage while also gaining the skills they would need to succeed in a rapidly changing world. It was important to Amina that the younger generation would not view their culture as something of the past, but as a living, breathing part of who they were. The program included field trips to historical sites, storytelling sessions with elders, and hands-on activities that involved traditional crafts and cooking. At the same time, students were taught the latest technologies and global trends, ensuring that they would be able to navigate the modern world with confidence.

As the cultural preservation program began to take shape, Amina also turned her attention to the valley's economy. The rapid pace of development had brought about an influx of new businesses and industries, but not all of them were beneficial to the local community. Many small businesses had been overshadowed by large corporations, and the valley's natural resources were being exploited without regard for sustainability. Amina knew that the valley's growth had to be sustainable, not just in terms of the environment but also in terms of its economy.

To address this, she launched an initiative to support local businesses and entrepreneurs. This initiative aimed to provide training and resources to small business owners, helping them to compete in the global marketplace without sacrificing their values. Amina worked closely with local artisans, farmers, and craftsmen, helping them to develop new products that could be sold in markets beyond the valley. She also established a micro-finance program that provided loans to young entrepreneurs, empowering them to start their own businesses and create jobs in their communities.

At the same time, Amina recognized the importance of environmental sustainability. The valley had always been known for its natural beauty, and she was determined to ensure that the land was preserved for future generations. She introduced policies that promoted sustainable farming practices, such as crop rotation and organic farming, and worked with local farmers to reduce their dependence on harmful pesticides and fertilizers. Amina also pushed for the protection of the valley's forests and waterways, ensuring that development projects did not destroy the natural resources that were vital to the valley's way of life.

Despite the progress that had been made, the valley's transformation was not without its challenges. As the population grew, so did the pressure on the land and its resources. There were disagreements over land use, and some people felt that their voices were not being heard in the decision-making process. Amina was faced with the difficult task of balancing the needs of the community with the demands of development. She worked tirelessly to ensure that all voices were heard, but it was not always easy to keep everyone satisfied.

One of the most significant challenges came when a multinational corporation expressed interest in building a large factory in the valley. The factory promised to create jobs and boost the local economy, but it also posed a threat to the environment and the traditional ways of life that the valley's people had fought so hard to preserve. Amina knew that this was a decision that would shape the valley's future for generations to come. She called for a series of public hearings, inviting experts, community leaders, and the general public to weigh in on the issue. After much deliberation, it was decided that the factory would be built, but with strict environmental regulations in place to ensure that the valley's resources were protected.

The decision was controversial, and not everyone was happy with the outcome. Some felt that the factory would bring too much change too quickly, while others believed that the valley's future depended on embracing the opportunities that modernization offered. Amina remained resolute in her belief that the valley could have both progress and preservation, but it would take careful planning and a commitment to finding solutions that worked for everyone.

As the years passed, Amina's leadership continued to shape the valley's future. The cultural preservation program flourished, and the valley's economy grew stronger, with more local businesses finding success in both national and international markets. The environment was better protected, and the community became more united than ever before. Yet, despite all the progress, Amina knew that the work was far from over. The valley was evolving, and it would continue to face new challenges in the years to come. But she was confident that, with the strength and resilience of its people, the Gboko Valley would continue to rise, just as it always had.

In the end, Amina's leadership was defined not just by the decisions she made, but by the way she brought her community together to shape their own destiny. She had learned from the leaders who came before her, and she had built on their legacy, ensuring that the valley's future was one that honored the past while embracing the possibilities of the future. The rise of great leaders from the Gboko Valley was not just a story of individuals—it was the story of a community that had learned to work together, to find common ground, and to create a future that was both prosperous and true to its roots.

8

Chapter 8

The sun set over the Gboko Valley, casting its warm golden rays across the expansive landscape, and signaling the start of another chapter in the region's history. The valley had undergone a significant transformation in recent years, but the journey was far from complete. New challenges and opportunities arose with each passing day, testing the resolve and adaptability of its people. Chapter eight was the continuation of this journey, the point at which the valley's leadership faced their most critical crossroads.

As the years progressed, the people of the Gboko Valley found themselves at a pivotal moment. The valley had prospered under the leadership of Amina, but a new generation of leaders had emerged, eager to carve out their own path and build upon the progress that had been made. Among these new voices was Emeka, a young visionary who had seen the world beyond the valley and had returned home with a passion for modernizing the region further. Emeka was determined to bring more technological advancements, expand the reach of education, and enhance the agricultural industry, but his approach was different from the strategies of previous leaders. His vision clashed with Amina's balanced approach, and the valley was soon caught in a tug-of-war between the two leadership styles.

Amina understood the importance of embracing the future, but she believed that the valley's identity could not be compromised in the pursuit of progress. Emeka, on the other hand, was more focused on the economic potential of the valley, seeing modernization as the key to unlocking new opportunities for growth. He argued that the valley could no longer rely solely on its traditional ways, and that the next step in its evolution was to adopt the latest technologies and global trends without hesitation.

The tensions between the two leaders began to grow, as Emeka's supporters rallied behind his message of rapid change, while Amina's followers stood firm in their belief that the valley should preserve its cultural roots. The people found themselves torn, unsure of which direction to take. The valley, once united under a common vision, now faced a division that threatened to unravel the progress they had made.

In the midst of this growing divide, a new issue emerged that brought the people of the valley together in unexpected ways. A powerful storm, more intense than any in recent memory, swept through the region, causing widespread damage to homes, farms, and infrastructure. The storm served as a reminder of the valley's vulnerability, and in its aftermath, the people realized that regardless of their differences, they would need to work together to rebuild and recover.

Amina and Emeka, despite their contrasting views, recognized the importance of setting aside their differences for the good of the valley. They called for a series of meetings to discuss the recovery efforts and to chart a path forward. The storm had not only destroyed physical structures, but it had also exposed the underlying weaknesses in the valley's infrastructure and disaster preparedness systems. The need for modernization in these areas became immediately apparent.

Emeka proposed the establishment of a comprehensive disaster management system, one that would integrate modern technology and global best practices in disaster response. He emphasized the need for early warning systems, better communication networks, and the use of drones and satellite technology to monitor the valley's environment in real-time. He argued that the valley's infrastructure needed to be reinforced to withstand future storms and other natural disasters, and that technology could play a pivotal role in protecting the people and their property.

Amina, though cautious about the rapid adoption of technology, acknowledged the importance of Emeka's ideas. She agreed that the valley's infrastructure needed improvement, but she stressed that the solutions should also take into account the community's needs and values. She proposed a hybrid approach, combining the use of modern technology with the traditional knowledge of the valley's people, who had lived with the land for generations and understood its rhythms and vulnerabilities. The elders, with their deep understanding of local weather patterns and ecological changes, had long been a source of wisdom in managing disasters, and Amina believed that their insights

44

should be integrated into any modern disaster management system.

As the recovery efforts began, the valley's leaders realized that the challenges they faced went beyond just the storm. The changing climate, rapid urbanization, and the pressures of globalization were all contributing to the strain on the valley's resources. The question was no longer just about economic growth or cultural preservation—it was about sustainability. The people of the valley needed to find a way to build a future that could withstand the challenges of the modern world while remaining true to their heritage and values.

One of the first steps toward sustainability was the development of a green energy initiative. The valley's abundant natural resources, including its vast stretches of farmland, rivers, and sunlight, made it an ideal location for renewable energy projects. Emeka's vision of modernization now included the harnessing of solar power, wind energy, and sustainable farming practices to reduce the valley's dependence on non-renewable resources. Amina, though initially skeptical, saw the potential in this new direction and agreed to support it, provided that it was done in a way that would not disrupt the community's way of life.

The green energy initiative was launched with a focus on train-ing local farmers and entrepreneurs in sustainable practices. Solar-powered irrigation systems were introduced to reduce water usage, and farmers were taught to grow crops that were more resilient to changing climate conditions. At the same time, wind turbines and solar panels were installed in key areas, providing renewable energy to power the valley's homes and businesses. The initiative was not only an effort to reduce the valley's carbon footprint, but it was also a way to create jobs and stimulate the local economy.

As the green energy initiative took shape, the valley's leaders continued to address the broader issue of sustainable development. Emeka and Amina worked together to create a blueprint for the future, one that would balance economic growth with environmental responsibility. They recognized that the valley's future depended on more than just technological advancements—it required a fundamental shift in how the people thought about their relationship with the land and their resources.

The creation of a sustainable agricultural model became the cornerstone of this new vision. Traditional farming techniques were revitalized, and modern methods were integrated in a way that enhanced, rather than replaced, the valley's agricultural heritage. Crop rotation, organic farming, and the cultivation of native plants were encouraged, and farmers were taught how to use technology to improve yields without damaging the environment.

Over time, the valley began to reap the rewards of its efforts. The environment became healthier, the economy grew more resilient, and the people found a renewed sense of pride in their traditions. Amina and Emeka, once at odds, had come to understand that their strengths complemented one another. The valley's success lay in its ability to embrace change while honoring its past.

But the journey was far from over. The challenges of climate change, global economic pressures, and the shifting dynamics of the modern world continued to loom large. Yet, the people of the Gboko Valley had learned an invaluable lesson: that true leadership was not about imposing one's vision on others, but about bringing people together to create a shared future. The leaders had learned that collaboration was key to overcoming adversity, and that only by working together could they ensure the valley's long-term prosperity.

As the years passed, the valley became a model for sustainable development, a place where progress and tradition coexisted in harmony. Emeka and Amina's leadership was a testament to the power of compromise and collaboration, and their work paved the way for future generations of leaders. The Gboko Valley, once divided by differing visions, had found a way to unite and thrive in an ever-changing world.

The rise of great leaders from the Gboko Valley was not just about individual accomplishments—it was about the collective strength of a community that had come together to build a future that was both prosperous and sustainable. The valley had proven that, with the right leadership, anything was possible. The journey was far from over, but the people of the Gboko Valley had learned that their greatest strength lay not in their differences, but in their shared vision for the future.

9

Chapter 9

The sky above the Gboko Valley was painted in deep shades of purple and red as the evening approached. The land, which had borne witness to countless struggles, triumphs, and moments of transformation, was once again ready for another phase of change. This time, however, the change was not simply about the evolution of infrastructure or the growth of technology—it was about the people themselves, their values, their unity, and their collective future. The valley, though small in comparison to the great cities of the world, had become a symbol of resilience, where the old and new had learned to coexist in a delicate balance. But as the winds of change blew through the region, it became clear that a new kind of challenge was emerging—one that would test the very soul of the Gboko Valley and its leaders.

As the valley's population grew and its industries flourished, a new generation of young people had risen to prominence. These young men and women, many of whom had gone abroad to study, returned with fresh perspectives on how to shape their community. However, their experiences outside the valley had instilled in them a desire to see the region advance rapidly and radically. They wanted the valley to leap forward, to modernize at an unprecedented pace. They saw the success of cities around the world that had embraced global trends, and they believed the Gboko Valley could do the same. But the elders, who had witnessed the valley's transformation from a quiet rural area into a bustling hub of agriculture and innovation, were more cautious.

The generational divide between the young and the old was becoming apparent. The younger generation, led by figures like Ugo, a charismatic businessman and entrepreneur, called for a complete overhaul of the valley's agricultural practices. They argued that the valley's reliance on traditional farming methods was holding it back. They envisioned a future where the valley could rival major agricultural powers, where advanced farming techniques, biotechnology, and even genetically modified crops could take center stage. Ugo's vision was one of rapid industrialization, where automation, large-scale farming, and corporate investment would transform the landscape.

On the other hand, the elders, led by figures like Nnadi, a respected elder who had lived through the valley's most turbulent times, held firmly to the belief that the valley's identity was rooted in its agricultural traditions. They feared that the new push for industrialization and technological innovation would erode the valley's cultural heritage and cause irreparable harm to the environment. Nnadi, who had seen firsthand the devastating effects of overexploitation in other parts of the country, warned that the valley's sustainability could not be compromised for the sake of unchecked growth. He advocated for a balanced approach, where modern advancements were introduced slowly and carefully, without disrupting the valley's way of life.

At the heart of this debate was a question that transcended politics or economics: What kind of future did the people of the Gboko Valley want to create? Was it a future where they could embrace the technological wonders of the modern world while holding on to the values of community, tradition, and environmental stewardship? Or was it a future where economic success and industrial progress would trump all other concerns? The people found themselves at a crossroads, unsure of which path to take.

It was during this time of uncertainty that an unexpected event brought the valley together in ways no one could have foreseen. A powerful multinational company, with interests in agriculture and biotechnology, arrived in the valley with an offer to invest in its future. The company promised to bring in state-of-the-art farming equipment, advanced irrigation systems, and genetically engineered crops that would increase yields and profitability. They also promised jobs, infrastructure, and a brighter future for the valley's youth. The proposal was enticing, and the valley's leaders knew that rejecting such an offer could mean missing out on an opportunity to propel the region into the future.

But the offer came with strings attached. The company's plans required large tracts of land, and many of these lands belonged to the farmers who had lived in the valley for generations. The company's proposal would force many small farmers to sell or lease their land, and it was unclear whether they would be able to maintain control over their livelihoods. Additionally, the company's operations would introduce large-scale, mechanized farming techniques that could eliminate many traditional jobs, leaving a significant portion of the population without work.

As the debate over the multinational company's proposal raged on, the people of the valley found themselves divided once again. The younger generation, led by Ugo, saw the company's investment as an opportunity to modernize the region and create jobs. They argued that the valley needed to evolve to stay competitive in a global economy. They envisioned a future where the valley could attract even more foreign investment, turning it into a thriving industrial hub that could rival any other region in the world.

The elders, however, were skeptical. They feared that the multinational company's interests were not aligned with the valley's long-term well-being. They questioned the wisdom of placing so much power in the hands of a foreign corporation, whose primary goal was to make a profit. They worried that the valley's resources would be exploited for short-term gain, leaving the people with little to show for their sacrifices. Nnadi, speaking on behalf of the older generation, warned that the company's presence could lead to the erosion of the valley's cultural identity and its environmental sustainability.

It was at this critical moment that a third voice emerged, one that had not been heard before. Amina, the once-respected leader of the valley, who had retired from active politics, came forward with a proposal that sought to unite the differing factions. Amina had spent years traveling the world, learning from other regions that had faced similar challenges. She knew that the valley's future could not be determined by the whims of either the young or the old. Instead, it had to be shaped by a collective vision that took into account both progress and preservation.

Amina proposed a compromise: a mixed approach that would allow the valley to benefit from the multinational company's investment while ensuring that its cultural and environmental values were preserved. She suggested that the company's investment be channeled into sustainable practices, such as organic farming, agroforestry, and renewable energy. She also proposed that the valley's small farmers be given a stake in the company's operations, ensuring that they had a voice in how the land was used and that they benefited from the economic growth that would result.

The proposal was not without its challenges. It required careful negotiations and a willingness to compromise on both sides. But Amina's vision of a balanced future resonated with many, and over time, the valley's leaders came to see the wisdom in her approach. The younger generation agreed to work with the elders to develop a sustainable model that would allow the valley to modernize without sacrificing its identity. The elders, in turn, agreed to embrace some of the new technologies, provided that they were used in a way that respected the land and the people.

The multinational company, seeing the unity of purpose in the valley's leadership, agreed to Amina's terms. The investment was made, but it came with strict guidelines that ensured the valley's farmers had control over their land and that sustainable practices were implemented. The company also agreed to collaborate with local leaders to create educational programs that would teach the valley's youth about sustainable agriculture, technology, and entrepreneurship. In this way, the valley could have its cake and eat it too—embracing progress without abandoning the values that had made it great.

As the years passed, the valley began to thrive once more. The new technologies brought with them increased agricultural yields and new industries, but they were tempered by a commitment to sustainability and community well-being. The valley's farmers, who had once feared the loss of their land, found that they had become partners in the region's success. The multinational company's presence, once seen as a threat, had become a catalyst for growth and innovation, but it had done so in a way that honored the valley's traditions and culture.

The story of the Gboko Valley was no longer just one of economic growth or political power—it was a story of resilience, unity, and the power of compromise. The valley had learned that the future was not something to fear, but something to shape together. And in that unity, it had found the strength to face whatever challenges the future might bring.

As the valley's leaders, young and old alike, looked out over the land, they knew that they had created something special. They had found a way to move forward without losing sight of who they were. And in doing so, they had set an example for the world—one that proved that progress and tradition could coexist, and that the greatest strength of all lay in the unity of purpose that bound them together. The valley, though small in the eyes of the world, had become a beacon of hope, a testament to the power of collective vision and shared responsibility.

10

Chapter 10

The morning sun rose slowly over the Gboko Valley, casting a golden hue over the lush landscapes that had long been the heartbeat of this community. The air was filled with the sounds of nature, the chirping of birds, the rustling of leaves in the wind, and the steady rhythm of life that had endured for centuries. This morning, however, there was an air of anticipation, for it marked the culmination of a journey that had been years in the making—the journey of transformation, unity, and the rise of leadership from the depths of the valley.

The leaders of the valley, both young and old, had gathered at the newly constructed community center in the heart of the valley. It was a moment of celebration, but also reflection, as they prepared to unveil the progress that had been achieved over the past several years. The world outside the valley may not have fully understood the significance of what was happening in this remote part of the country, but for those who lived here, it was a victory that would resonate for generations to come. It was the triumph of a community coming together to shape its own future, a future defined by the fusion of tradition and modernity, of sustainability and progress.

Ugo, the young businessman who had once led the charge for industrialization, stood at the front of the gathering, flanked by Nnadi, the elder who had once cautioned against rapid change. Their presence together, symbolizing the union of the old and the new, was a testament to the hard work that had gone into bridging the gap between the two generations. The valley, it seemed, had learned to embrace its diversity—both in terms of age and thought—and had used that diversity to forge a path forward.

Ugo, now in his thirties, spoke first. His voice, once full of youthful ambition, had matured over the years, carrying with it a wisdom borne of experience. "Today, we stand at the crossroads of a new era," he began, his words echoing through the room. "When we first set out on this journey, we were faced with a difficult choice: to cling to the past or to embrace the future. But as we've seen, the future is not something that can be built by abandoning the past. It is something that is created when we bring together the best of both worlds."

He paused, allowing his words to sink in. "We have not lost our traditions," he continued. "We have strengthened them. Our farmers are using the latest technologies to grow crops more sustainably, while still honoring the land that has fed us for generations. Our youth are learning to innovate, but they are also learning to respect the wisdom of our elders. Together, we have built something that is truly special."

The crowd nodded in agreement, and a wave of pride washed over them. It was clear that Ugo's words were not just those of a businessman, but of a man who had come to understand the value of community, culture, and collaboration.

Nnadi, the elder who had once opposed some of the more radical changes, now stepped forward. His weathered face, marked by years of experience, held a smile that spoke volumes. "When I first spoke out against some of the changes that were proposed, it was not because I didn't believe in progress," he began, his voice strong but calm. "It was because I had seen too many communities lose themselves in the pursuit of progress. I had seen the land exploited, the culture forgotten, and the people left behind. But today, I stand here proud. Proud of the leaders we have become. Proud of the decisions we made, and the path we walked together."

His words were met with applause, and many in the crowd were moved by the depth of emotion in his voice. Nnadi had not only witnessed the valley's past struggles but had also been a part of its triumphs. His experience had been a guiding light for the younger generation, and now, it seemed, his hopes for the future had been realized.

"The valley has become a symbol of what can be achieved when we work together," Nnadi continued. "It is a symbol of resilience, of unity, and of the power of community. We have shown that the old and the new can coexist, that the wisdom of the past can guide the innovations of the future. And for that, I am deeply grateful."

The crowd erupted into applause once more, and for a moment, the entire valley seemed to hold its breath, united in its pride. It was a rare moment of collective triumph, one that had been earned through years of hard work, difficult conversations, and, above all, mutual respect. The leaders of the valley, in their own ways, had come to understand the importance of compromise, of listening to one another, and of finding common ground.

The celebration continued throughout the day, with speeches, music, and dances that reflected the diverse cultures of the valley. People from all walks of life came together to celebrate their shared achievements, and the energy in the air was palpable. It was a celebration of the valley's progress, yes, but it was also a celebration of the journey itself—the journey that had brought the people together, that had tested their resolve, and that had ultimately strengthened their bonds.

As the sun began to set, casting its final rays across the valley, Ugo and Nnadi found themselves standing together, looking out over the land they had both fought for. The valley had changed in many ways, but in its heart, it remained the same. It was a place of hope, of possibility, and of a future that was still being written. Ugo turned to Nnadi, a thoughtful look on his face.

"We've come a long way," he said, his voice quiet. "But there's still so much more to do."

Nnadi nodded, his eyes fixed on the horizon. "There will always be more to do," he replied. "But that is the beauty of leadership—the journey never truly ends. As long as we remain true to our values, to our people, and to our land, we will continue to rise. The valley will continue to rise."

Ugo smiled, a sense of peace settling over him. He had once believed that the future could only be built by tearing down the past, but now he understood that the future could only be built by honoring both the past and the present. The valley had become a place where the old and the new could coexist, a place where progress was not defined by the abandonment of tradition but by the integration of both. The rise of great leaders from the Gboko Valley had not been a story of revolution, but of evolution—a story of people coming together, learning from one another, and working toward a common vision.

As the stars began to twinkle in the night sky, Ugo and Nnadi stood in silence, knowing that their work was far from over. The valley was not perfect, but it was a place where hope had been rekindled, where leadership had been redefined, and where the future was once again within reach.

The sun may have set on this day, but the journey of the Gboko Valley was only just beginning. With the strength of its people, the wisdom of its leaders, and the unity of its community, the valley was poised to rise once more. And as the night embraced the land, the valley's promise lingered in the air—silent but undeniable, like the whisper of the wind through the trees, a reminder that the best was yet to come.

www.ingramcontent.com/pod-product-compliance
Ingram Content Group UK Ltd.
Pitfield, Milton Keynes, MK11 3LW, UK
UKHW020705060225
454761UK00011B/371